# ANGELS

# ANGELS

## A Short Biblical Survey

James B. Currie

**JOHN RITCHIE LTD**
CHRISTIAN PUBLICATIONS

40 Beansburn, Kilmarnock, Scotland

ISBN 0 946351 90 2

Copyright © 1999 by John Ritchie Ltd.
40 Beansburn, Kilmarnock, Scotland

Typeset by John Ritchie Ltd., Kilmarnock
Printed by Bell & Bain Ltd., Glasgow

# Contents

# Author's Foreword

The revelation which God has given of Himself to mankind is threefold. Firstly God has revealed Himself for all to see in the handiwork of His creation. "For the invisible things of Him from the creation of the world are clearly seen, being understood by the things that are made, even His eternal power and Godhead" (Rom 1.20). Secondly God has spoken to mankind in His Son, Jesus Christ. About 2,000 years ago, God, in the person of His Son, was manifested in a human body, sinless and in every way perfect. That revelation is full and complete. Thirdly, in the written record of these divine manifestations, found in the Holy Scriptures, God has given His last word to men of every age. Alongside the testimony of the material universe to the power and wisdom of the Creator, and the record of the life of Christ on earth, the Scriptures give us an authentic insight into the spirit-world that is not found elsewhere. These Scriptures therefore include much information about those magnificent spirit-beings we call angels.

Until quite recently, this subject was usually greeted with skepticism by most unbelievers; especially those who pride themselves in their intellect. Nor was it a topic calling for the attention of the majority of Christians either. But *the angels of God* occupy an important place in what God has to say to us. The roles they play are an  integral part of the story of redemption.  Whilst God has seen fit to limit what we may know about them, what has been revealed should cause us to bow humbly in worship before their Creator, and ours.

During a lifetime of ministering God's Word to believers throughout Japan, questions concerning the angels had to be considered and answered. Eventually, a series of articles was written for the believers' magazine known as *The Word*. These articles were, of course, written in Japanese and were published in book form in 1994. They have also had a gracious acceptance in both the Dutch and the Chinese languages, hopefully to the profit of those who have read them.

That they were originally magazine articles will soon be noted by the attentive reader. This will be seen in the measure of repetition and, perhaps, disjointedness marking this little book now published in English. Some kind friends have attempted to eliminate these weaknesses, perhaps without too much success. The fault lies with the author and not with his helpful editors. I trust that the Lord will overrule in grace so that the evident faults mentioned will in no way detract from any spiritual benefit the reader may receive. In any event, may God, through our Lord Jesus, the Captain of the Lord's Host, receive all the glory.

Tokyo, Japan
September 1999

CHAPTER 1

# Introduction

The Biblical subject of *Angels* is interesting, informative, but generally neglected in evangelical circles. In days long gone, men such as Thomas Aquinas and John Calvin wrote at length on the theme, but in more recent years not too much of a definitive nature has been written. On occasions in oral ministry the subject has been touched upon in a passing manner but, generally, seldom spoken of or written about in a way calculated to give an insight into the breadth of divine revelation found in the Scriptures for our learning. The small amount of written material available, often being of an experiential and subjective nature, does not help much towards an understanding of these personages who sustain a lofty position before their God. That the angels do enjoy a station of majestic grandeur and privilege may be understood by the fact that man, the glory of God's physical creation, "crowned with glory and honour" is, nevertheless, said to have been "made a little lower than the angels" (Ps 8.5).

Any reliable concordance will show that angels are mentioned, one way or another, some two hundred and seventy five times in the Scriptures. We who hold that "all Scripture is given by inspiration of God, and is profitable for doctrine, for reproof, for correction, for instruction in righteousness: that the man of God may be perfect, throughly furnished unto all good works" (2 Tim 3.16-17), should be aware of this. A subject spoken of so often by the Holy Spirit cannot be neglected by the saints without great spiritual loss being incurred.

Perhaps one of the main reasons for the neglect, and at times, ignorance of this wonderful topic is that down the ages much superstition has attached itself to human notions regarding these heavenly hosts. This has led to all sorts of grotesque representations of the angels so that many a non-believer has dismissed the entire subject as something springing from medieval ignorance and irrationality. They claim to do so upon the grounds of intelligent investigation. In view of the many strange notions propounded by religionists in ages past, they are hardly to be blamed for that. But the Word of God being Christ-centered, the believer, in his reading and study of God's self-revelation, seeks to find "Christ in all the Scriptures", as the title of an earlier publication puts it. However, the intermediary beings - for this is what the angels of God are - whilst taking on an aspect of an incomparably lesser importance than the incarnate Maker Himself, also call for diligent study on the part of the Lord's people.

Based on what Scripture has revealed, all Christians accept the existence of angels but many feel that they have little to do with our immediate situation in the physical realm. Indeed, there are those who, even after careful search of the Word of God, are of the opinion that angels have nothing to do with us in this present dispensation characterized as it is by the special presence and activities of the Holy Spirit. Such teachers would tell us that angelic ministry is limited to the ages when "The Kingdom" is manifested in various ways. As we shall see, the Biblical references to these superb servants of God are to be found more often in the New Testament than in the Old, suggesting that they are very much a part of God's dealings with men even in our day and age when "The Kingdom" is seen in mystery form (Matt 13.11).

The studies that follow are in no way exhaustive but they may prove helpful by making us more aware of the relevance and of the vast scope of angelic ministry, even in the present era. This day of grace is, without question, peculiarly that of the Holy Spirit. We are confident that all the spiritual blessings God has bestowed upon us in Christ are made good to us in the power of the Spirit. That being the case, it almost seems as if angelic ministry is superfluous as far as the believer of the church age is concerned. We are most reluctant to allow anyone or anything to encroach upon the blessed work and prerogatives of God's Spirit, and rightly so. For instance, it does cause confusion in the minds of some when we see angels employed to make known the mind of God to men in such a way as is recorded in Luke 1. There Gabriel appeared to Zacharias and to Mary with the announcements of the birth of John and of the Lord Jesus. In Matthew 1 it was the *the angel of the Lord* who appeared to Joseph with a similar announcement. At the same time it was, apparently, the Holy Spirit who, in filling Elizabeth, revealed to her that Mary was to be the mother of her Lord (Luke 1.41). These and other matters must be taken into consideration.

The Bible is basically the *History of Redemption*. Therefore, angels are to be seen only in relation to the purpose of God towards man in this connection. Religious mythology in every part of the world has much to say about angels, or spirit beings, almost all of it based on unholy imagination. The Bible, by contrast, is quite reticent in what it does reveal about them, in spite of its numerous references to this subject. However, many insights are given as to their origin, their present ministry, and what lies before them in God's eternal purpose. But given man's propensity to worship such creatures (Rev 22.8), God has seen fit to allow us only a slight but very instructive glimpse of a subject that touches on eternity past and future.

**An Outline**

An orderly approach to our subject is required. In order to appreciate somewhat the different facets of truth contained in some of the scriptural references to angels, the following outline will be followed and may be a help.

1. Angels - their identity

2. Angels - their dignity

3. Angels - their ministry

4. Angels - their destiny

CHAPTER 2

# The Identity of Angels

**Their Creation**

While there are many Jewish traditions concerning the creation of angels, only the Word of God may be relied upon to give a true account of this momentous event. Although mere human curiosity will not be satisfied with the relatively scant information the Scriptures provide, more than enough is given to enable us to appreciate the exalted place they occupy in the divine order of creation. Some ancient writers held that they were created during the six days of Genesis 1. Taking Psalm 104.2-3 to refer to the first day of creation, some have suggested that v.4 of the Psalm, "Who maketh His angels spirits; His ministers flames of fire", indicates their creation on the second day. But any sequential order supposedly found in these verses is immediately upset by the words that follow; "Who laid the foundation of the earth, that it should not be removed for ever". This statement must be linked with what is revealed in Genesis 1.1: "In the beginning God created the heavens and the earth". That they were created by God is clearly stated in the words of the Levites in their recounting of God's goodness to Abraham and his seed: "Thou, even thou, art Lord alone; thou hast made heaven, the heaven of heavens with all their host" (Neh 9.6). While these words could be taken to mean all the stars and planets of the physical realm, yet what is further stated, "the earth and all *things* that are therein, the seas, and all that is therein" must refer to the living creatures of these environs that are preserved by the Lord. In a similar fashion the words "the host of heaven worshippeth Thee", can only refer to the angels. Angels are, on numerous occasions, spoken of as "the host of heaven" (e.g. 2 Chron 18.18; Luke 2.13).

**The Morning Stars**
The Lord Himself told Job that "the morning stars sang together and all the sons of God shouted for joy" when the foundations of the earth were laid (Job 38.7). If we are to look for the time of their creation in the Genesis record, it might be best to see them brought into being when, as already quoted, "God created the heavens and the earth", but of that no certainty exists. Whatever interpretation may be given to this, and subsequent verses, we are justified in believing that angels were present with their songs of joy and praise when God acted in creative power, furnishing the heavens and the earth before Adam was made a living soul by the breath of his Creator. The conclusion that they were created, together with the heavens of Genesis 1.1, perhaps is inferred in Psalm 33.6: "By the word of the Lord were the heavens made and all the host of them by the breath of His mouth."

**The Sons of God**
The saints of this and a past dispensation are called "the sons of God" (Hos 1.10; Gal 4.6). This privileged position is enjoyed by the believer as the result of the work of redemption, but the angels are "sons of God" by virtue of their creation. The words of the Lord Jesus in Matthew 22.30 show that they neither marry nor are given in marriage. No record is given of angelic birth or death. It appears that each of these beings, who may differ from one another in rank and in function, comes as a unique and direct creation from the hand of God. The angels' existence is entirely spiritual, in contrast to man who is composed of spirit, soul and body (1 Thess 5. 23). In what form they exist is a mystery to us at present but on occasions, and in keeping with divine

commissioning at the time, they are able to appear in human form. These appearances do not imply a permanent appropriation of human shape. "A spirit hath not flesh and bones" (Luke 24.39) are the words of the Lord Jesus in resurrection, which show that the spiritual nature of angels is different again to that which resurrected saints will possess. We are reminded by Paul that these "our lowly bodies" (NIV) will one day be changed and fashioned like unto our Lord's own body of glory (Phil 3.21).

Just what it means to exist in a purely spiritual form is not ours to know by experience, but the Scriptures show that such beings are not limited by any of the phenomena of the physical realm. Note how swiftly Gabriel came in answer to Daniel's prayer (Dan 8.21). The fact that one angel slew one hundred and eighty five thousand Assyrian warriors in one night, underscores the mighty power with which they are, at times, endowed (2 Kings 19.35). Imagine the dreadful havoc that would have been caused if the Lord had called for the "more than twelve legions of angels" who were prepared to come at His command while in the garden of Gethsemane (Matt 26.53). Twelve legions, or more than sixty thousand angels (*Vine's Dictionary of OT. & N T Words*, p.329), swiftly coming to the aid of the Lord would have left, not only the mighty Roman empire, but the whole world a desolated ruin. What a sight it must have been to these angels to see their Lord submitting to the taunts and torments of His puny creature man and willingly allowing Himself to become subject to death itself – this so that His very tormentors might have the hope of salvation. Therein was a display of amazing grace far beyond anything the angels could have imagined.

The rationalizing of worldly philosophers notwithstanding, it would appear that a class of beings such as is portrayed in Scripture as angels, is necessary to round out creation as we know it. In matters vegetable, each tree or plant bears exactly the same characteristics as all the others in its species.

"A rose is a rose is a rose" and this *ad infinitum*. In the animal kingdom, the herd instinct is prevalent to a very large degree, but each animal does, at times, show individual traits. On the other hand, it is evident that in men "the herd instinct" is greatly subdued and individuality very pronounced, though almost everyone will react in exactly the same way to a given set of circumstances, e.g. to the cry of "fire" in a crowded building. The Word of God portrays angels as beings individually created by their Creator with absolutely no trace of a collective instinct whatsoever. Thus, it might be said that for the completeness of creation, the existence of such beings is almost mandatory.

We have noted that the *when* of their creation may not be stated dogmatically. This is not so with regards to *why* they were brought into being. The apostle Paul states unequivocally that the Lord Jesus was both the agent and the reason for their creation. "His dear Son ... the firstborn of every creature: For by Him were all things created, that are in heaven and that are in earth, visible and invisible, whether they be thrones or dominions, or principalities or powers: all things were created by Him and for Him: And He is before all things and by Him all things consist (or, are held together)" (Col 1.13-17).

### Their Excellent Names

Angels are said, at least by inference, to have "an excellent name" (Heb 1.6). It is almost certain that the words of Psalm 97.7, "Worship Him all ye Elohim", refer to them. Only four angels are named in God's Word but the meaning of their names does emphasize the excellence of their station or their power. He who was appointed by God as "the anointed cherub that covereth" (Ezek 28.14), is also called LUCIFER, "son of the morning" (Isa 14.12). Whilst both these chapters present problems to the honest exegete, yet, almost unanimously, reverent teachers of God's Word see in the prophets' words no mere hyperbole, but a superlative description of a being

16

whose excellence goes far beyond that of the earthly kings of Babylon and Tyre. Lucifer, whose name means "morning star" is said to "seal up the measure of perfection, full of wisdom and perfect in beauty" (Ezek 28.12, JND). His beauty was such that only the magnificence of the most precious jewels could convey it to the human mind. Perfect in his ways from the day he was created, his original link with the holy throne of God is illustrated in the two cherubim covering the lid of the mercy seat. His exalted station was that of "the cherub that covereth" (see Ex 25.20).

It would appear that of all the created beings, this "son of the morning" stood pre-eminent. The fact that "iniquity was found in him" as the result of his gigantic pride (1 Tim 3.6), in no way detracts from the "excellent name" he bore. Lucifer was "lifted up because of his beauty" (Ezek 28.17), and with a fivefold declaration of self will, sought to become the ruler of all "the stars (angels) of God", and thus become "like the Most High" (Isa 14.13-14). What a tremendous contrast to the One who being in the form of God thought not that equality with God was something to hoard selfishly for Himself alone, but was made in the likeness of man, and taking the form of a slave, humbled Himself even unto the death of the cross (Phil 2.7-8).

MICHAEL, the archangel, whose name means "who is like God", and GABRIEL, "God's mighty one", are two other angels named in God's Word. They bear "an excellent name", not only in a literal way, but in the divine commissions entrusted to them. To a lesser degree, each of the "innumerable company of angels" (Heb 12.22) bears such an excellent name also. Stamped with and reflecting a likeness to their Creator, they are "the holy angels" (Matt 25.31), "the elect angels" (1 Tim 5.21), and, probably, "the holy ones" (Jude 14).

The fourth angel who is named in the Scriptures is ABADDON or APOLLYON. He appears in Revelation 9. He falls into a different category from the others already mentioned. Difference of opinion exists as to whether or not this angel is Satan. It would appear that he is, at least, a prince of the underworld, an evil personage inspired by Satan. But in either case, nothing is taken away from the fact that his name means 'destroyer' and that, having the hordes of locust-like creatures at his disposal, his is an awesome power. Strictly speaking this angel belongs to a later part of our study.

By way of contrast, the Lord Jesus is said to have "by inheritance a more excellent Name than (the angels)" (Heb 1.4). They are "sons of God" as the result of their creation, just as Adam was (Luke 3.38) but the divine declaration concerning our Lord Jesus is "Thou art My Son" (Heb 1.5) in His eternal sonship, and by virtue of what has been termed the eternal generation. This non-scriptural phrase must not be misunderstood to mean "descendent from" as in generation by birth. It is the theologian's device to give expression to the unparalleled and eternal relationship which the Lord Jesus sustains as the "only begotten Son" (John 3.16). Other explanations of these difficult words quoted from the second Psalm are forthcoming, but it is true that there never was a moment in all eternity when the divine declaration, "Thou art My Son" was not the unique expression of the relationship between the Father and the Son. If the term proves inadequate in expressing what it is meant to convey it could be said that it is the best we have. To limit the words "Thou art My Son, this day have I begotten Thee" to 'the crises of the incarnation', that is to say to the incarnation itself, to the resurrection and the priestly consecration of the Lord, hardly seems to do justice to the momentous truth involved. In either event no created being, be he ever so great as to character and position, can say as did the Lord Jesus, 'Glorify THY Son that the Son also may glorify Thee' (John 17.1 - the grammatical signs in The Newberry Bible warrant this emphasis). The words "Thy Son" and "the Son" speak of an intimacy and a relationship *nonpareil* with the Father that the Lord Jesus alone sustains and does so world without end.

The divinely inspired writer to the Hebrews speaks much of the angels in chapter one. He does so to show that by "eternal generation" (v.5), in His universal adoration (v.6), in His regal manifestation (v.8), and in His final exaltation (v.13), the Lord Jesus bears a "more excellent Name" than do any of the angels of God.

MICHAEL'S name appears five times in the Scriptures. He is called "the archangel" and appears to have a special responsibility to the nation of Israel, particularly as to their defence (Dan 10.13; 12.1; Rev 12.7-12). His supreme position among the angels notwithstanding, he shows a complete dependence upon His God when contending with Satan (Jude 9). In this he gives to Satan the respect due to him, in spite of his fallen state.

The name GABRIEL appears four times and his special assignments have to do with revelations to the people of God. In Daniel 8, his message concerns the "end times". In the chapter following, he is the agent through whom the momentous prophecy of the "seventy weeks", pertaining to Israel's history, is revealed. In the New Testament, he is used by God to instruct Zacharias and Mary concerning the birth of John the Baptist and of the Lord Jesus Himself (Luke 1). Gabriel is called "the angel of the Lord" (Luke 1.11). Even though there is a hiatus of five hundred years between the end of the Old and the beginning of the New Testament, he takes up where he left off in Daniel and is again sent by God to convey facts concerning God's purposes in redemption.

Various references throughout Scripture reveal the following. There are "angels of judgment" (Gen 19) and there are heavenly "watchers" (Dan 4) who have authority over governments and the governors of this present world. The "angel of the abyss" (Abaddon), as noted, appears in Revelation 19 while an "angel of the waters", an angel controlling outpoured fire (ch.16) and "angels of churches" (ch.2 & 3) are also spoken of.  These combined scriptural references would lead us to the conclusion that, in multitudinous ways, angelic beings act with authority as God's agents in government and in grace in the control of the cosmos and with regards to God's people.

## The Cherubim
*Not Merely Symbolic*

The angels are further identified by the various ranks or positions they occupy.  The first of these beings to appear on the pages of Scripture are, of course, the cherubim of Genesis 3.  The word "cherubim" appears on numerous occasions in the Old Testament, particularly in the book of Ezekiel where it is used nineteen times. It is used but once in all of the New Testament (Heb 9.5).  Here we have the meaningful phrase, "the cherubim of glory".  It is not so easy to determine the meaning of the word itself.  One suggestion, among many, is that it means "to till" or "to plough" and may indicate their diligence in service for God.  Both Ezekiel in his prophecy and John in the Revelation refer to these magnificent beings as "the living creatures" (Ezek 1; Rev 4, JND).  What is said of them signifies that, with all the zealous energy of life itself, they fulfill their service for God without interruption.  Many writers accept the view that they are symbolic rather than actual beings of the very highest rank.  While they do embody in their persons much that is representative or symbolic, to view them as actual beings seems to be more in keeping with what has been revealed about them.  As has already been shown, Satan is spoken of as "the anointed cherub" before his fall. This underlines the fact that the cherubim are superior and are individual beings.  It is hardly likely that that which is merely symbolic would be spoken of as being "anointed".

What is recorded concerning them in Scripture should give us reason to marvel at the transcendent ministry and position they are appointed to. God is spoken of as "dwelling (or sitting) between the cherubim" (Ps 80.1; 99.1). This fact is illustrated in the covering and the veils of the tabernacle. Woven into the very fabric of these veils were representations of the cherubim, so that God's dwelling place in the midst of the nation of Israel was characterized by the pervading portrayal of their station. This is further seen in the lid of the mercy seat where two cherubim, forming an intrinsic part of that lid, are linked with the demands of absolute holiness symbolized in the ark of the covenant. Apparently four in number, the cherubim are attendant upon the very throne of God (Rev 4.6). In their persons they give expression to the inscrutable ways of God in grace and in government with regards to man, "for the spirit of the living creatures was in the wheels" (Ezek 1.21, Revised AV). In their essential being, the cherubim are *expressive* of the holiness of God (Gen 3). They are *protective* of the throne of God (Rev 4) and they are *indicative* of the divine work of redemption (Ex 25).

Being four in number, their representation of divine attributes is meant to be seen as universal. The four faces which each of the cherubim possesses have been interpreted in various ways. If, as has been suggested, they are meant to personify divine attributes, then "the face of a man" would speak of superior intelligence, that of "the lion" of complete sovereignty, the "face of an ox" would remind us of that divine patience which knows no limit, and "the face of an eagle" would indicate the heavenly activity put forth on man's behalf. In keeping with Ezekiel 1, John also writes of these four characteristics (Rev 4.7). He further agrees with the prophet in showing that these living creatures were "full of eyes" (Ezek 1.18; Rev 4.8). That is to say, they were characterized by an almost divine omniscience. A cautionary note must be sounded here. Such is the incomparable superiority of the cherubim as created intelligences that Ezekiel, in depicting these beings in their relationship to the "visions of God" which were given him, was compelled to use the words "likeness" and "appearance" no less than twenty-five times in chapter 1 alone. It is evident that words cannot, in any way, approximate the transcendent glory seen by Ezekiel, but the facts as recorded are in keeping with Paul's experience when he, too, had to say of the man caught up into Paradise, "'he heard unspeakable words which it is not possible for man to utter" (2 Cor 12.14, AV mar.). Yet most significantly, the prophet does record "this was their appearance; they had the likeness of a man" (Ezek 1.5).

### The Four Faces Seen in the Gospels

From ancient times, the four faces of the cherubim have been linked with the four Gospels: that of the lion to Matthew, the Gospel of the King; the face of the ox with the servant's Gospel of Mark; the face of a man to Luke's record which sets forth the "Man Christ Jesus" in all His perfection; and the Gospel of John, showing distinctively the heavenly origin of God's Own Son, is linked to the eagle characteristic. These cherubim, or living creatures then, as to their essential being, portray many divine attributes to the whole creation, but, in actual fact, no mere creature, no matter how magnificent, can ever hope to be a perfect manifestation of the divine character. The four Gospels are a reminder that only a divine Person could reveal God in all His Glory. "No man hath seen God at any time; the only begotten Son, which is in the bosom of the Father, He hath declared Him" (John 1.18). This statement could be posited only of the Lord Jesus.

Interestingly, in the first chapter of Ezekiel, one of the faces is that of an ox but in 10.14 it is changed to that of a cherub. In the second reference this is the first one of the four mentioned. Symbolically, the meanings are probably very similar. In chapter 1, in conjunction with the call of the prophet, that which suggests patient service, the ox is noted, as is the overall appearance "the likeness of a man" (vv.6, 26). In chapter 10 the context is that of the glory departing from God's House on earth. The picture of patient earthly service is replaced by that which is suggestive of a heavenly and glorified ministry.

Again, the superlatives used to describe these magnificent "living creatures" are there to show the infinite superiority of the Man who possesses all the divine attributes and manifested them in "bodily form", whether on earth or presently as glorified in heaven (Col 2.9).

## The Seraphim
### Different Ranks of Beings

From antiquity, as many as nine different classes of angelic beings have been recognized by the use of various designations found in the Scriptures. Already noted is that hierarchy called "the cherubim". A further rank of these beings is called "the seraphim". They, too, occupy a place of great privilege and dignity. Many of their characteristics are similar to those of the cherubim and, because of this, are often thought of as being one and the same. The word "seraphim" appears only twice in Scripture (Isa 6.2,6) but what is recorded concerning this class of angels would lead to the conclusion that they also have a separate and distinct entity and a divinely-given commission. Both cherubim and seraphim give expression to the holiness of God. The former rest not day and night as they proclaim, "Holy, holy, holy, Lord God Almighty, which was and is, and is to come" (Rev 4.8) and the latter cry one to another saying, "Holy, holy, holy is the Lord God of Hosts; the whole earth is full of His Glory" (Isa 6.3). If these descriptions are to be taken literally, then Ezekiel 1.6 poses a dilemma since the cherubim are there said to have "four wings" while the "living creatures" in Revelation are shown to have six. If, on the other hand, the number of wings spoken of is seen to be symbolic then the problem disappears, as does the necessity for identifying as the same these two groups of angelic beings.

As has already been suggested, the four wings of Ezekiel

1, symbolize the universality of the cherubim's representation of deity, while the six wings of Isaiah 6 and Revelation 4 would symbolize the sense of awe, the humility and the energy with which such beings serve their Creator. What a lesson is to be learned in this by mere mortals who, even in service for God, are often marked by pride and self-sufficiency. Both the seraphim and cherubim share in the outstanding characteristics mentioned. The cherubim and seraphim alike cover their faces in the presence of effulgent glory. Feeling their own inadequacy, they cover their feet while they hasten to do the bidding of their Lord and Creator. Oh, that we could be more like them as we serve the Master here.

### The Characteristics of the Seraphim

The special characteristics of the seraphim mark them as different, if not in rank, certainly in their ministry. The cherubim are linked to the throne of God and that, in some way, as protectors of its holiness, but the seraphim are linked to the altar in Isaiah 6.6. Related to their service to the throne of God, the cherubim demand that the sinner approach God by way of sacrifice. In a similar manner, the ministry of the seraphim illustrates the need for cleansing for those who would serve such a God of holiness. The name "seraphim" means "burning ones". The same word is used to describe the fiery serpents of Numbers 21.6 where the all-consuming holiness of God was served in judgment by the serpents. From this we would conclude that, just as the name "the living ones" is used to describe the cherubim in their unflagging energy in service for God, so the name "the burning ones" would indicate the intensity and unquenchable zeal the seraphim show in their divinely appointed ministry in keeping with that holiness. They are, as one writer has put it, "inflamed with love to God" and are marked by a reverent humility allowing nothing to hinder or interrupt the speedy obedience to the commission they have been assigned. Once more they give to us a wonderful example as servants of the

Most High. We, who are marked by mortality and weakness in all that we do, ought to be even more aware then they are of the reverence and humility called for as we, by grace alone, are privileged to serve the Lord in our sphere as they do in theirs.

Both cherubim and seraphim cry, "Holy, holy, holy is the Lord God Almighty." No doubt this indicates the triune character of the God of whom they speak. The threefold repetition is also meant to express the deep perfection of God's holiness, and may also be an expression of that holiness which characterizes the Lord God Almighty in (1) His sovereign dealings with angelic beings in the sphere of the spirit, (2) His mighty work in the physical creation, and (3) in all His gracious ways with men here on earth. In whatever way we explain this reverent acknowledgment of God's holiness, we should be much more cognizant of our own imperfections and shortcomings in service for God as we contemplate the love and holy zeal of these heavenly beings.

One further thought must be noted in connection with the ministry of the seraphim. The cleansing agent used to put away Isaiah's deeply felt inadequacies was a "coal from off the altar". Again, the action must be seen to be symbolic. The altar and the burning coals would speak of the redeeming work of Christ and all its effects. Not only does that glorious work bring pardon for the sinner, it also removes personal uncleanness and makes the believer fit to serve the God of his salvation. In view of what "the live coal from off the altar" represents and the assurance it must have given God's servant, it is no wonder that Isaiah's response was, "Here am I, send me" (Isa 6.8).

## Other Designations

As previously indicated, linked to the time of their unique creation, the angels are called "MORNING STARS" in Job 38.7. The title is a declaration of the brightness of the glory with which they have been endowed. In this they give expression to the character of their infinitely more glorious Lord who is called "the bright and morning star" (Rev 22.16).

There are also the "WATCHERS" of Daniel 4.13-17. These appear to be in the same category as the "WATCHMEN" (keepers) of Isaiah 62.6. Such angels act in an administrative capacity for their God with regards to the political sphere here on earth, especially as these affairs have to do with the people of God. How closely linked is their relationship to the political happenings of this world may be seen in Daniel 4. One of these "watchers" carries the edict from "The Most High". The word he carries from heaven is, "hew the tree down and destroy it". Nebuchadnezzar, perhaps the greatest world ruler known until that time, is thereby sent forth to the fields to act the part of a dumb beast. It may be inferred from this that political events are directed by God at the hands of such agents.

Further, some angels have apparently a special relationship to individual nations in the rise and fall of worldly empires. These are called "PRINCES" (Dan 10.13, 20; 12.1). Satan is named "the Prince of the power of the air" (Eph 2.2), "the Prince of demons" (Matt 9.34) and "the Prince of this world" (John 14.30). All of these titles, no doubt, reflect the majestic position Satan originally occupied when first created and point to the relationship he continues to sustain in happenings in this world. But, again, by wonderful contrast, the Lord Jesus is called "the Prince of life" (Acts 3.15).

Other spiritual beings are termed "THRONES, DOMINIONS, PRINCIPALITIES and POWERS" (Col 1.16), once more indicating, apparently, various ranks among the angels. These titles speak of exalted positions, power and authority and, withal, the ability to execute government as delegated by their divine Lord. Such, then, is, in part, the identity of such glorious beings, who, in their absolute perfection, set before us object lessons of untiring zeal for God as they serve Him with becoming reverence and humility.

CHAPTER 3

# The Dignity of Angels

The essential dignity of the heavenly hosts may be seen in at least four ways. Some of these points have already been touched upon but may be developed a little further.
1. Their pre-incarnate Lord identified Himself with their station.
2. They are linked to the holy Throne of their Creator.
3. They are authoritative agents for God.
4. Their ministry to the Lord while He was here on earth.

**1. The Pre-incarnate Lord identified Himself with the angels.**
There can be no reasonable doubt that the words "the Angel of the Lord" or "the Angel of God" which appear almost seventy times in the Old Testament, refer clearly, most of the time, to a unique and special individual. While some disagree, most expositors see that the appearances of "the Angel of the Lord" are *Theophanies*, or representations of God to man, prior to the incarnation of the Lord Jesus. This belief explains many portions of Scripture which otherwise would remain enigmatic and difficult.

The conditions surrounding the fourteen Theophanies found in the Old Testament would lead to the conclusion that "the Angel of the Lord" is a truly divine Person. The first occasion is found in Genesis 16 when "the Angel of the Lord" appears to Hagar who "called the name of the Lord who spoke to her, 'Thou God seest me'" (v.13).

It is "the Angel of the Lord" who, "swearing by Himself", says to Abraham, "In blessing will *I* bless thee and in multiplying *I* will multiply thy seed" (Gen 22.16-17). The writer to the Hebrews ascribes this oath given to Abraham to the God who cannot lie (6.17-18). "The Angel of God" who spoke to Jacob in Genesis 31 calls Himself "the God of Bethel" (v.13) and "the Angel of the Lord" who appeared unto Moses in Horeb "in a flame of fire" also identifies Himself as "the God of thy father, the God of Abraham, the God of Isaac and the God of Jacob" (Ex 3.2-6).

To the children of Israel, "the Angel of the Lord" says, "I made you go up out of Egypt ... and I said I will never break my covenant with you" (Judges 2.1). Other similar incidents occur in the experiences of Balaam (Num 22), Gideon (Judges 6), Manoah (ch.13), David (2 Sam 24), Elijah (1 Kings 19), Ornan (1 Chron 21), Isaiah (Isa 37) and Zechariah (Zech 1). We have limited these references, in this instance, to the occasions where the words "the Angel of the Lord" are actually used, but there are other occasions recorded in which a divine Person appears as an angel or in human form, again indicating that the Angel of the Lord is not just one of a kind, but the only One of His kind. Thus the Almighty Creator Himself dignified the habitation of the angels by revealing Himself to His own as "the Angel of the Lord".

With these Scriptural references before us, what depth of meaning is then found in the words of Psalm 34.7-8: "The Angel of the Lord encampeth round about them that fear him, and delivereth them. Oh taste and see that the Lord is good; blessed is the man that trusteth in Him."

"The Angel of the Lord" possesses all the attributes of deity. In Exodus 23.21, the Lord God of Israel says, "My Name is in Him." Everything that the ineffable Name of Jehovah expresses is to be found in the One God calls "Mine Angel" (Ex 23.23). He is also called "the Angel of His presence" (Isa 63.9). The Lord who had bestowed great goodness on the house of Israel says of Him, "in all their affliction He was afflicted, and the Angel of His Presence saved them: in His love and in His pity He redeemed them: and He bare them and carried them all the days of old".

Two other interesting titles are given to the Angel of the Lord. In Job 33.23-24, the Lord says, "If there be a messenger (angel) with him (mankind whose soul draws near unto the grave), an interpreter, one among a thousand to shew unto man his (the angel's) uprightness: Then He (God) is gracious unto him and saith, Deliver him from going down to the pit: I have found a *ransom*." Some may have difficulty with the interpretation of this verse as given in brackets, but of the main thrust of the words themselves, likely little argument will be given. In Malachi 3.1, He is also called "the messenger (angel) of the covenant", the One who will fulfill the covenant, purify the sons of Levi and cause the offering of Judah and Jerusalem to be pleasant unto the Lord. These two titles, "the Ransom" and "the Angel of the Covenant", point to the two advents of the Lord Jesus. These help us to identify the One who is so often called the "Angel of the Lord". He came first of all to give His life a ransom for many (Matt 20.28). He comes a second time to fufill all the promises of the covenant (Heb 9.20,28).

Such is the dignity of these holy beings that the Lord Himself, prior to His being "made flesh and tabernacling among us", (John 1.14) deigned to reveal Himself as "the Angel of the Lord".

## 2. They are linked to God's Throne

The dignity of their position is further seen in their close relationship to the Throne of God. Apart from the unique relationship the cherubim bear to the Throne (Rev 4.6), Gabriel says to Zechariah, "I am Gabriel that stand in the presence of God" (Luke 1.9). The drama of Redemption, as revealed in the New Testament, opens with a man on earth being brought into the intimate secrets of heaven by angelic ministry. Five hundred years earlier, Gabriel appeared to Daniel under similar circumstances; that is, at the time of the evening sacrifice, to announce the seventy weeks determined upon Israel to make an end of transgression and usher in the righteousness of the ages. This would be accomplished by the cutting off of Israel's Messiah (Dan 9). In Luke 1, Gabriel announces the Messiah's birth, thus setting in motion the process to bring about salvation that had been promised long before.

In similar fashion to Gabriel, the seven angels of Revelation 8, who are charged with the trumpet judgments, also "stand before God"; as does "another angel", that is, one of the same kind as the previous seven (8.2-3). This latter angel is seen by many as being the Lord Jesus, but since the pronoun implies "another one of the same kind" and that the Lord Jesus is never referred to as an "angel" anywhere else in the NT, it seems more appropriate to view him as an angelic servant possessing Christ-like characteristics. At any rate this "angel" gives power to the prayers of the suffering saints of that period. The result is that as the seven angels prepare to sound their trumpets of judgment and as the "seven last plagues" (15.1) are poured out upon the earth dwellers, the cries of those who said, "How long, O Lord, holy and true" (6.10) are answered by the ministry of the angel who casts the fire from off the altar upon the earth. Then as the last of the angels pours out his bowl of wrath upon the earth "Voices and thunderings, and lightnings and earthquake" accompany his action (16.17-18). In Daniel 7.9-10, it is said "thrones were cast down, and the Ancient of days did sit, whose garment was white as snow ... A fiery stream issued and came forth from before Him: thousand thousands ministered unto Him, and ten thousand times ten thousand stood before Him: the judgment was set, and the books were opened". It is indeed awe-inspiring to consider that when the Lord is revealed in His glory, He will be accompanied by these "angels of His might" (2 Thess 1.7).

In the book of Revelation, one such angel challenges the universe (ch.5); another angel exercises authority over the earth in chaos (ch.10) and still another avenges on Babylon the blood of martyrs and saints (ch.18).

### 3. They are authoritative agents for God

That their power is not intrinsic but is delegated to them, makes it no less remarkable. Acting for God, they are agents of both grace and government. From the words of the author of Hebrews, and in keeping with other Scriptures, we may conclude that the present cosmos is in subjection to angelic administration. But in the redemptive purposes of God, the world to come has not thus been placed in subjection to them (Heb 2.5). It is not beyond possibility that the vast reaches of space, populated by the billions of stars and planets, are administered by the angels in some way for God. This is what C.S. Lewis envisages in his book "*Out of the Silent Plane*". Mere speculation perhaps, but it is difficult to believe that such numberless spheres have been created without purpose and lacking orderly administration.

As we have seen, angels are in control of all nature, at least as it pertains to this earth. The angels of fire, water, wind, etc. of Revelation 16 are engaged in assuring that the ultimate purpose of God is fulfilled. At Sinai, no less than ten thousand "Holy Ones" attended the giving of the Law (Deut 33.2; Acts 7.53; Gal 3.19). The Law, thus ordained at the hand of angels, revealed the holy character of the God of Israel. Moreover, in their capacity as "Watchers", they supervise the movements of nations, and thereby the sovereign prerogatives of God are enforced (Dan 4.23; 12.1). This will be seen in more detail later in our study.

### 4. Their Ministry to the Lord on Earth

It would appear that angelic activity increased during our Lord's sojourn on earth. Announcing His birth (Luke 2); ministering to Him in the wilderness (Matt 4); attending the events of His passion (Luke 22); proclaiming His resurrection with an utter contempt for death's power (Matt 28); and forming part of His train in ascension glory (John 1.51). In this latter Scripture, the angels are seen "ascending and descending upon the Son of Man". That is to say, they are completely under His control and at His disposal. Their ministry to the Lord is made even more interesting by Paul's words, "seen of angels" (1 Tim 3.16).

In just such ways is the dignity of these holy beings emphasized. They are called both sons and servants. What they enjoy by virtue of their Creator's handiwork, we enjoy as the fruits of redemption. Indeed, our position in Christ is even more dignified and intimate than theirs. "Beloved, *now* are we the sons of God, and it doth not yet appear what we shall be; but we know that, when He shall appear, we shall be like Him; for we shall see Him as He is" (1 John 3.2). Again, these superb servants of God serve as an example for the redeemed who also are called upon to serve with the dignity of "sons of God".

CHAPTER 4

# The Ministry of Angels

## Instructed by the Work of Grace

There are two statements concerning the angels which will be considered in more detail in the following pages. They are the words "seen of angels" (1 Tim 3.16) and "unto the angels" (Eph 3.10). Their link to the down-stooping of the Lord Jesus and to the divine work of amazing grace manifest in the formation of the church which is Christ's body, leaves no doubt as to their depth of meaning. Similarly, the further phrase of 1 Corinthians 11.10, "because of the angels", is also worthy of careful evaluation. Sadly, this latter statement is often ignored as unimportant by many who have taken in hand to expound the First Epistle to the Corinthians.

Since Paul's words concerning the "lengthening" hair and the head covering, in connection with the women of the Corinthian assembly, are thought to have been merely the custom of the day, they are, usually, set aside as being of no consequence to the Christian of the present age. It is remarkable that so many believers of this latter part of the twentieth century can treat so lightly what has been the uniform custom of the "churches of God", almost without exception, for over 1900 years. In the apostle's day, as in ours, men were required to cover their heads in the Jewish synagogue, but for the women, this was optional although an almost universal practice. In the idols' temples, it was not mandatory for either man or woman to be covered, so that, far from following the custom of the day, Paul was introducing something new, and that by "commandment of

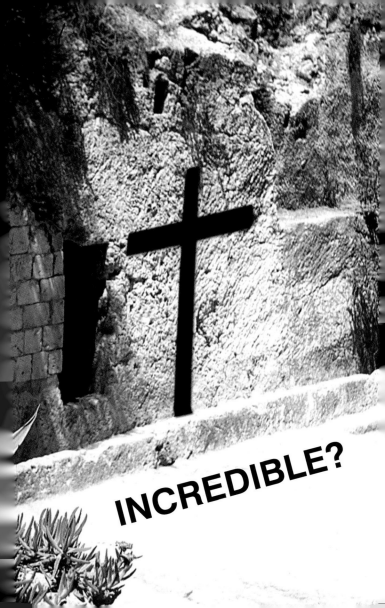

INCREDIBLE?

Picture an ancient courtroom in Caesarea on the Mediterranean Sea. The defendant in the dock is Paul, the first Christian missionary: the judges, Festus a Roman governor, and a puppet king called Agrippa. What are the charges? Accusations had been that the prisoner's sermons were unsettling the nation. In particular, it outraged the Jews that one of the main topics of Paul's preaching was his insistence that Christ had been raised from the dead; "Jesus, which was dead, whom Paul affirmed to be alive" (The Bible: Acts 25.19).

Paul conducted his own defence, and before long, a question thundered around the courtroom; **"Why should it be thought a thing incredible with you, that God should raise the dead**?" (Acts 26.8). It is nothing to the Almighty to effect resurrection; it is not outwith His ability; He is supreme in power. On the first Easter morning, the tomb in which the body of Jesus had been laid was vacant; "He is not here: for he is risen" (Matthew 28.6). Hundreds testified to it because they saw Him with their own eyes (1 Corinthians 15.5-9). An early statement of Christian conviction was this; **"we believe that Jesus died and rose again**" (1 Thessalonians 4.14). Why did He die? The Bible's answer? "Christ died for our sins" (1 Corinthians 15.3). His death was a sacrifice

...us, our sins. We all have sins and they need to be ...rgiven and the threat of their punishment has to be removed. To make that possible Christ died for our sins.

Why was He raised? Among other reasons, to provide a living Saviour, someone who is "able to save" (Hebrews 7.25). By repentance, and faith in that Saviour, the blessings of forgiveness and salvation are received, for "whosoever shall call upon the name of the Lord shall be saved" (Romans 10.13).

Statistics can be misleading but there is one statistic against which there is no argument; ten out of ten people die. It might be the result of an accident. It could be a wasting illness. It may be the sudden malfunction of a major organ. In every case there is an inevitable winner; the Bible says, "we must needs die" (2 Samuel 14.14), it also poses this crucial question, **"If a man die, shall he live again**?" (Job 14.14). In other words, will there be resurrection for us as there was resurrection for Christ? Yes, there will. Believers in Christ will be raised; those who reject Him will also be raised. These resurrections will be at different times and will have a different outcome. The first will take place when He comes again, and the outcome will be eternal bliss in heaven (1 Thessalonians 4.13-18). The second will be at the end of world history, and will result in an appearance at His judgment throne, and from there, eternal punishment (Revelation 20.11-15).

These are huge issues; they affect you for eternity; it is vital to make the right response to the living Saviour. Receive Him now by repentance and faith, and in the ultimate you will experience "the resurrection of life" (John 5.29).

"Why should it be thought a thing incredible with *you*, that God should raise the dead?"

JH

the Lord". This is a fact that ought to be more widely recognized than it is.

Again, careful consideration of Paul's words will show that the teaching and practice acknowledged universally by believers in every age but our own cannot be ignored without spiritual detriment to those who disregard it. The assembly in Corinth, and by inference, in every other place, represents the divine work of restoration. What was lost in the garden of Eden as the result of man's sin, God intends should be restored in the "companies of the redeemed". The natural order of the material creation, of which the Lord Jesus is appointed sole and sovereign Lord, is completely disrupted in man's sinful society. This disruption stems from Eve's deception by Satan (1 Tim 2.14). She was led by the serpent's guile to step from God's appointed place for her. Of her sin, in which Adam willingly participated, it could also be said that "she kept not her first estate". In the companies of the saints called "the churches of God", God's original design is seen restored. The Lord Jesus is given His rightful place in the midst of His own. The outward expressions of this grand truth are to be found in the behaviour and dress of both man and woman. While in "the church which is (Christ's) body" there "can be neither male nor female" (Gal 3.28), these distinctions are very much to the fore in the local gatherings of the saints. Thus, the men are taught to wear their hair short and with uncovered head to participate in the privilege of public prayer and ministry. The believing woman is called upon to have her hair long, to wear a covering in all the gatherings of the assembly, for whatever purpose, and to "learn in silence with all subjection" for, says Paul, "I suffer not a woman to teach nor to usurp authority over the man" (1 Tim 2.11-12). This interdiction extends even to public prayers: "I will therefore that *the males* pray in every place". For these injunctions, the apostle gives four clear reasons in 1 Corinthians 11.

(1) For the woman to be uncovered during times of prayer

or prophesying is to dishonour her head (v.5); the "head" referring to man in his natural but divinely appointed sphere. The woman, "praying or prophesying" uncovered is not acknowledging the God given headship of the man.

(2) Nature itself teaches that, for a man to have long hair and a woman to have her hair short, intentionally, is repugnant (vv.14-16).

(3) None of the churches of God had any other custom than what Paul here advances (v.16).

(4) Last, but by no means least, and intimately connected to the subject in hand, these symbols of simple and unquestioning obedience and recognition on the part of redeemed men and women are said to be *"because of the angels"* (v.10).

In view of what is being propounded here, would it be overstating the meaning to suggest that angelic ministry in grace and glory is made all the more solemn and glorious by what they are called upon to witness of the divine work in redemption and its results?

The angels, with much scriptural justification, are said to be "guardians of the order of creation" and are "interested spectators" of God's ways with man. The willing obedience of God's people, brought about by God's grace in salvation and seen in the outward symbols of covered head and lengthening hair of the sisters, is a further means whereby the angels are enlightened as to divine purposes. Lest there be any objections, it should be noted that it is "lengthening hair" of which Paul speaks. The *Linguistic Key to the NT* interprets the word *kamao* "to let one's hair grow" (p.424), and the *Greek Dictionary to the N T* supplementing *Strong's Exhaustive Concordance to the N T* gives the meaning "to wear tresses (of hair)" (word No. 2863). In Paul's day, homosexuality was often expressed by men in their long hair. Many, alas, in our days also follow this unnatural practice (although it would be incorrect to accuse every man who sports long hair as being also involved in this unnatural and unscriptural practice). With the angels as interested eyewitnesses being instructed by the work of God's grace among men, every spiritual believer, man or woman, will acknowledge that the things Paul writes are, as stated already, "the commandments of the Lord" (1 Cor 14.37).

## Agents in the Work of Judgment

A solemn note is sounded in Revelation 14. In spite of grace in infinite measure and the divine forbearance, man continues in his rebellion. This is headed up in his future acceptance of the great rebel, the Man of Sin. Fearful judgment is meted out upon "the earth dwellers". The angels are divine agents in this (Rev 6 -19). Those who "worship the beast and his image; and receive his mark in his forehead or in his hand ... shall be tormented with fire and brimstone in the presence of the holy angels, and in the presence of the Lamb" (14.9 -10). Apparently, the angels will be associated with all the momentous events that ensue after the coming of Christ to the air to rapture His own to be with Himself. "The Lord Himself shall descend with a shout, an *archangelic-like voice* and the trump of God" (1 Thess 4.16 - italics a literal revision). At the judgment seat of Christ, they will appear as onlookers. This appears to be implied in the words of Luke 12.8. They will accompany the Lord when He comes again into the world and they will be called upon to offer Him worship at that time (Heb 1.6). But it will be in the very presence of the holy angels that vengeance will be meted out upon all the worshippers of the Beast. A further divine means is thus shown in the education of the angels.

Perhaps it is with this also in view that Paul writes to Timothy, "I (solemnly) charge thee before God and the Lord Jesus Christ, and the elect angels, that thou observe these things without preferring one before another, doing nothing by partiality" (1 Tim 5.21). Neither familial nor friendship ties, nor indeed any other hidden motive, is to interfere with the faithful setting forth of "sound doctrine" and in the call for suitable behavioural responses thereto. Such is the weight of responsibility incumbent upon those who publicly minister the Word of God, that they are to be constantly aware of the "holy angels" who are keenly interested in and are observing the work of divine grace at this present time. Even more so shall the presence of the angels be required in that grand day of review when "every man shall receive his own reward" (1 Cor 3.8).

**Participants in the Paeans of Praise**
The ministry of angels is both heavenly and earthly. It is one of glory, of grace and of government. Towards God, it is indicative of the glory of God's person and purpose (Ps 103.12-21); "All His angels praise Him" (Ps 148.2). None are silent and their praise is continual since "they rest not day or night" in their offering of worship (Rev 4.8) which is universal in aspect (Isa 6.3). When the glory of God filled Solomon's Temple, the priests were unable to "stand before God" (2 Chron 5.14), but, in spite of effulgent glory and of impending wrath, angels are seen "standing before God" and the altar in heaven (Rev 8.2-3). With regards to events on earth, their ministry is seen to be both administrative and assertive. The present order of the cosmos is under their controlling agency and as they minister to all who "are about to inherit salvation" (Heb 1.14, lit. trans.) the promises of God for His Own, at least as far as physical protection is concerned, are carried out. Then, too, in relationship to the Lord's tabernacling here on earth, theirs was an attentive and an extensive ministry. From the moment they heralded His birth they ministered to Him in various ways. Linked to Him in Gethsemane, they also supervised the empty tomb before they confirmed His ascension. They will also accompany Him on His return in Glory.

Even though theirs is such an exalted estate and although they are agents of divine wrath and vengeance, in a future day they will be subservient to redeemed man. That they will add their voices to the praises of the redeemed is made clear in Revelation 5.11-12. Their participation will, of course, be different, but they, too, will share in the benefits accruing from the glorious work of the Lord Jesus. In Hebrews 12.22-24, they are said to be "an innumerable company of angels gathered in festal array" or "gathered to keep a feast" as some translators suggest. They are spoken of as "elect angels" (1 Tim 5.21). When the "great city, the Holy Jerusalem" descends out of heaven from God, twelve angels are at the gates (Rev 21.12). It is thus made plain that angels, whilst not directly the beneficiaries of the grace of redemption, are nevertheless not excluded from the blessings resulting from the cross work of our Lord Jesus Christ. One of the lesser known but extended results of God's glorious work of redemption is the guarantee which Calvary provides, that never again will sin and rebellion defile or disrupt the ranks of these holy beings. To suppose otherwise is to imply that the whole process of redemption might need to be repeated. Such a thought is grotesque in the extreme. What the Lord accomplished in His death is eternal salvation for all who believe. An equally eternal assurance is provided for the elect angels, that they who have been set aside in God's sovereign purpose, will never again know the devastation sin once brought among them. This great festal gathering of angels is, consequently, eternal in nature.

The new song of the redeemed, which will never grow old, will be "Thou art worthy ... for Thou hast redeemed us to God by Thy blood" (Rev 5.9). The backdrop to that anthem will be a vast chorus, the voice of an innumerable company of angels around about the Throne and the living creatures. Their chorus of praise is seen to be in harmony with the "twenty-four elders" who, in the view of the present writer, represent the redeemed of this age of grace and present the prayers of the saints in that heavenly scene. These "prayers of the saints" include, then, the redemptive song of praise (v.9) and the further anthems of the large heavenly host are given in vv.11-14. The number of this vast host defies expression in human language. With a loud voice, they (angels, living creatures and redeemed men) say, "Worthy is the Lamb that was slain to receive power, and riches and wisdom and strength, and honour and glory and blessing". Together with the whole of creation, they will ascribe unending praise to the God of their creation for the mighty work He wrought in redeeming man to Himself, and for the eternal preservation that the angels enjoy.

We, as believers, have ever been plagued by a limited vision - never more so than in the affluent days of our times. A clear understanding of the magnificence of these superb beings in their character and service for God should help us appreciate in a much deeper way, the value of spiritual things. The "innumerable company of angels", who never have and never will taste of salvation's precious fruits, serve their God in the full energy of their whole being. Their example of zeal and fidelity is ours to follow.

CHAPTER 5

# The Destiny of Angels

So far, we have noted that the Scriptures identify the angels in at least two ways. They are seen as worshippers in the heavenly sanctuary and, as "ministering spirits" they act as messengers or agents for God, in errands of grace and government. Further, their dignity is that of "Holy Ones" who, probably and even more than the anointed kings and prophets, as companions of Christ (Ps 45.7) albeit as His servants, communicate the mind of God, execute the will of God and administer the judgment of God. They know nothing of the experiences of birth, sickness, death or decay. In spite of this, they, too, are the subjects of divine discipline with a view to bringing about the eternal purpose of the Godhead as to their destiny.

In the New Testament, certain things are said of the angels that help us understand how these beings are presently being instructed in divine things. Especially noteworthy are the following four statements, three of which have already been referred to in chapter 4:

'seen of angels' (1 Tim 3.16),
'unto the angels' (principalities and powers) (Eph 3.10),
'because of the angels' (1 Cor 11.10),
'in the presence of the angels' (Luke 15.10; Rev 14.10).

These scriptures respectively present the angels in general as (1) interested spectators, (2) inquiring observers, (3) instructed learners, and (4) intelligent witnesses of the ways of God with men on earth.

## 'Seen of Angels'

It is interesting to note that, among the most profound statements concerning Christ made by Paul in the New Testament, are the words of Philippians 2.5-11 and I Timothy 3.16. The apostle's purpose was not doctrinal in either place, but practical. In the former, it is that the mind of Christ might be formed in the Philippian saints, and in the latter, it is that men might know how to behave themselves in "the church of the living God". The phrase, "seen of angels", in the context of 1 Timothy 3.16, is extremely broad in its scope, covering the incarnation in all its varied aspects. From the time they announced His coming into manhood they were privileged to minister to their Lord in various ways, even to the extent of strengthening the Lord in some mysterious way at the time of His agony in Gethsemane. (see Matt 1.20; 4.11; Luke 22.43). Every step of the way from the incarnation to the ascension the Lord appears to be attended by one or more of these beings. The only occasion when their ministry was not called for was when the Lord Jesus was left alone on the cross. In spite of the fact that the twelve legions of their number were readily available to do His bidding, the Lord did not call upon them at that time. With what wonder and awe must the angelic host have witnessed all that it meant for their Creator to empty Himself of the outward manifestation of His glory, to take the form of a servant and to be manifested in the likeness of mortal man. The down-stooping of the Creator to manhood would have been wonder enough, but they also saw His humbling of Himself so that, in obedience to the will of His Father, He might taste death, even the death of the cross. In this, they witnessed a unique outpouring of love and grace that they never could have seen by any other means. But the story did not end there. They also witnessed His triumphant resurrection out from among the dead and His glorious ascent back to the Father's throne. Nothing in the collective experience of these unnumbered hosts could have prepared them for what to them must have been completely inexplicable, the Mighty God allowing Himself to be "made a little lower than the angels" so that He might "taste death for everything" (Heb 2.9).

## "Unto the Angels"

To Paul was given the inestimable privilege of filling up the divine revelation (Col 1.25). The topmost stone, as it were, is found in the Ephesian epistle, and, to an extent, also in Colossians. The subject in the first of these two letters is "the church which is (Christ's) body, the fullness of Him that filleth all in all" (Eph 2.23). Out from the multitudes of those "who were dead in trespasses and in sins", "the children of disobedience and of wrath" (Eph 2.1-3), whether Jew or Gentile, God has "in love predestined (the believers of this present age) unto the adoption of sons" (Eph 1.5). According to "His good pleasure which He hath purposed in Himself" (Eph 1.9). He has created for Himself an eternal paean of praise (Eph 2.10), "a holy temple" of which the Lord Jesus is the chief corner stone (Eph 2.20-21). This mighty work of "grace abounding" is in keeping with the eternal purpose of God which He purposed in Christ Jesus our Lord, "to the intent that *unto the principalities and powers* might be known by the church the manifold wisdom of God" (Eph 3.10-11). The wisdom of God is many-faceted. There are profound depths to it that could never have been plumbed by any angel, nor by all the angels combined, had it not been for the work of Calvary and the manifest purpose of God towards man in it. "In the ages to come, God will show the exceeding riches of His grace towards us through Christ Jesus" (Eph 2.7), but even now "unto the principalities and powers", that is to say, *"unto the angels"* is being shown the magnitude of God's gracious and many-faceted wisdom in the church which has been constituted "the filling up of Him who fills all things". No doubt with similar thoughts in mind, Peter writes: "Which things the angels desire to look into" (1 Pet 1.12). The means whereby God brings into existence this eternal monument to His grace and wisdom is "the preaching of the gospel with the Holy Spirit sent down from heaven". It is probably no exaggeration to say that, on the occasions when the gospel is preached, angelic beings give it their fullest attention, even when men do not. This adds lustre to Paul's words in Ephesians 3.8 when he speaks of preaching "among the Gentiles the unsearchable riches of Christ".

### "Because of the Angels"

Just as the church "which is Christ's body" is the means whereby the manifold wisdom of God is made known "unto the angels", in a similar manner are the "churches of God", the assemblies of the saints, used as a divine classroom to instruct the angels in the ways of God with men. In 1 Corinthians 11 Paul deals with God's order in the material creation. In keeping with what had already been taught to the Corinthian believers, he writes: "I would have you know that the head of every man is Christ; and the head of the woman is the man; and the head of Christ is God" (v.3). These words relate to God's original purpose in man's creation. Man, as God's regent, was placed at the head of all the physical domain, while woman was placed alongside Adam as "a help" suitable to him (Gen 2.20-23).

In harmony with this divine order in the physical realm, the woman was placed in subjection to the man. In exactly the same way, the man, although endowed with supreme authority in his own sphere, was also placed in subjection, and that to Christ. We are told that "all things were created by and for" our Lord Jesus Christ (Col 1.16). But the divinely constituted order in the material cosmos was disrupted when Eve, who was intended to be a help suitable for the man, was deceived by Satan's infamous slander of her Creator. Sin thus entered man's society in precisely the way it had in the realm of the angels, that is to say, by way of rebellion against God and His Word. There the similarity ends. The result of angelic rebellion was instant and irrevocable judgment. "The angels that sinned – (were) delivered into chains of darkness to be reserved unto judgment" (2 Peter 2.4). By gracious contrast, the occasion of man's original sin became a vehicle for the display of God's loving mercy. The nakedness of both man and woman in the garden was covered as the result of a sacrificial death, and the first intimation of God's redemptive purpose was given. The angels, in amazement, might well have asked, "What is man that Thou art mindful of him or the son of man that Thou visitest him?" (Ps 8.4-6; Heb 2.6).

The process of redemption, thus hinted at in the garden of Eden, reaches its climax in what angels were called upon to witness, their Creator and God, humbling Himself to become liable for the sin and guilt of creature man. His purpose was that man's transgression would be blotted out, thereby drawing the sinner to Himself in the bonds of an inexplicable love. The result of this "great salvation" wrought by divine Persons is wonderfully unique. All three persons of the Godhead were involved in it. This is expressed succinctly in the words of Hebrews 10.14: "Christ, who through the eternal Spirit offered Himself without spot to God". The believing sinner, turning from his path of sin and rebellion, now, most willingly, subjects himself to the mind of God, both as an individual, and, in company with others of his fellow-saints. In this way an outward expression is given to divine order once again restored; this in the sphere where defiance of God and His Word are endemic.

This outward expression of subjection to the mind of God takes three forms in the conduct and deportment of both the believing man and woman. For the male believer, it is seen in his short hair, and, in all the public gatherings of the people of God, in his uncovered head; then, also, in his divinely-granted privilege of participating audibly in the spiritual exercises of the assembly. By these outward demonstrations, he acknowledges that "the head of every man is Christ". For the believing woman, her long hair and, in the assembling of the saints, her covered head and her subjective silence are, for her, the outward symbols of the truth of the apostle's words, "the head of the woman is the man". Specifically, with regards to the woman's covering, Paul says; "For this cause ought the woman to have a sign (of being under authority to the man) on her head *because of the angels*" (1 Cor 11.10). Thus, to angelic observers is a further lesson taught. In dealing with sinful man in grace, God has brought about a complete change of attitude and behaviour so that, entirely apart from legal requirements, mortal man bows willingly in subjection to His Lord. Such an object lesson to the angels is inestimable and could only have been produced by God's work of redemption in the souls of men. This was brought about by the death of our Lord Jesus Christ. It is difficult to understand why so many Christians ignore or make light of this symbolism that is so full of meaning and beauty and that, until very recent years, was accepted as normal practice by Christians of every ecclesiastical persuasion.*

### "In the Presence of the Angels"

No doubt with such thoughts before him, Paul lays a solemn charge upon his younger friend and co-worker, Timothy. "I charge thee before God, and the Lord Jesus Christ, and *the elect angels,* that thou observe these things (pertaining to assembly order) without preferring one before another, doing nothing by partiality" (1 Tim 5.21). As has already been suggested this solemn charge demands that Timothy apply the teachings to all believers without prejudice, in view of the fact that the angels are interested in, and are observers of, the God-glorifying results of this salvation.

Not only so, but the apostles who suffered so much for the

---

*See Ritchie Booklet - *The Head Covering* - where this subject is fully discussed.

cause of Christ, and no doubt others with them, are set forth as the tail end of the triumphant procession and as a spectacle to the whole cosmos. Rank upon rank of both men and angels are caused to witness the faithful response in the hearts and lives of these servants to God's grace in salvation. In spite of being "appointed to death" and becoming "the off-scouring of all things" (1 Cor 4.9-13) these devoted ministers of God give the angels (and the world of men) one more illustration of what God has accomplished by grace and in the death of His Son.

In the divine purpose, angels can never participate in God's salvation. Even in the many doxologies of praise they offer to God, no note of thankfulness is sounded because of salvation. This is in contrast to redeemed man who can and does sing the new song, "Thou wast slain and hast redeemed us unto God by Thy blood" (Rev 5.9). However, they do appreciate what it means, to some extent at least. The Lord Jesus tells us "there is joy in the presence of the angels over one sinner that repenteth" (Luke 15.10). It may be that the words "in the presence of the angels" are synonymous with v.7 where the Lord says, "There is joy in heaven over one sinner that repenteth", but surely the implication is that the angels are not excluded from heaven's joy in the salvation of men.

With regard to the discipline or instruction of angels, another point should be mentioned and it is most solemn. In Revelation 14.9-11 it is recorded of the Beast-worshippers that "they shall drink of the wine of the wrath of God, which is poured out without mixture into the cup of His indignation and they shall be tormented with fire and brimstone in the presence of the holy angels, and in the presence of the Lamb". The grace and forbearance of God in infinite measure has been scorned and rejected by those who receive the mark of the Beast. In the judgment of these "earth-dwellers", the angels are again made to understand the depth of God's holy hatred and indignation against sin. In this fashion are the angels instructed, not only concerning His infinite love and mercy, but also as to God's immutable righteousness. Both to man and to angels, Paul's words in Romans 11.33 are fraught with deep emotion and meaning: "O the depth of the riches both of the wisdom and knowledge of God! How unsearchable are His judgments and His ways past finding out".

CHAPTER 6

# The Final Judgment of Angels

Both Peter, in his Second Epistle, and Jude give a threefold fearsome example of God's holy hatred of sin and of its judgment. Some have suggested that one or other of these Biblical authors used the letter of his fellow-writer as the basis for his own work, resulting in mere duplication. That there are many similarities in the two short letters, no one will deny, but the differences are just as numerous, as can be seen in the examples of judgment referred to. One basic difference is that of the dissimilar viewpoints the authors have with regard to false teachers. Peter warns those to whom he writes: "There shall be false teachers among you" (2.1) and "There shall come in the last days scoffers, walking after their own lusts" (3.3). Jude, on the other hand, tells his readers that such have already appeared. "These be they who separate themselves, sensual, having not the Spirit" (v.19). This, he says, is in keeping with "the words which were spoken before of the apostles of our Lord Jesus Christ" (v.17). It is evident that Jude is referring to conditions as they were at the time of writing, whereas Peter saw them as yet future.

## "The Angels that Sinned"

Moreover, whilst Peter uses "the angels that sinned", "the old world" of Noah's day, and "the cities of Sodom and Gomorrah" as examples of judgment (2.4-6), Jude speaks of the destruction of unbelieving Israel in the wilderness, alongside "the angels which kept not their first estate" and "Sodom and Gomorrah and the cities about them" (vv.5-7) as his three part example. For our purpose, the point of contact between the epistles is that of the angels, their sin, and subsequent judgment. It is certain that both authors refer to the same events.

There are many triplets found in Jude's epistle. One of these, the unbelieving Israelites, the angels who left their own habitation, and the cities which went after strange flesh, is used to show the character and ultimate judgment of "ungodly men" who "deny the only Lord God, even our Lord Jesus Christ" (v.4). As his three examples show, they are marked by unbelief, rebellion and immorality. Peter has also a twofold object before him. By referring to "the angels that sinned", "the old world" of the antediluvian era, and "Sodom and Gomorrah", Peter shows that "the Lord knoweth how to deliver the godly out of the temptation and (at the same time) reserve the unjust unto the day of judgment to be punished" (2.8). The object of the authors, the order they follow and the actual illustrations they use, all show distinct differences.

With regard to the angels, three things are said by both Peter and Jude. Peter speaks of them as "the angels that sinned". This corresponds to the words of Jude, "the angels which kept not their first estate but left their own habitation"(or, "left their own homes", NIV). There is absolutely nothing in either of these statements to suggest that anything is intended other than the original sin of rebellion which Satan and his angels committed. They were assigned "a principality" and a "habitation". That is to say, they had been given a sphere of authority and a place of existence all of their own which they left. This they did when they were caught up in Satan's attempt "to be like the Most High"

(Isa 14.14). Satan "defiled his own sanctuaries". This came about by the "unrighteousness of his traffic" (Ezek 28.18, JND). Everything that is said by both Peter and Jude concerning the sin of angels is explained forthrightly by the record in Isaiah and Ezekiel. The result of their iniquity is that God "hath reserved (them) in everlasting chains under darkness" (Jude 6), or, in Peter's words, "God ... cast them down to hell and delivered them into chains of darkness" (2.4). In spite of the fact that many authorities prefer the word "pits" or "caverns" to "chains" in Peter's account, Jude's use of the word "bonds" (RV) should indicate what is really meant. Paul uses exactly the same word "figuratively, to indicate a condition of imprisonment" (Phil 1.7, *Dictionary of NT Words*, W.E. Vine). Since they are called "chains or bonds of darkness", it should be evident that a figurative meaning is intended. Peter's statement that "God ... cast them down to hell" appears to complicate this explanation, but not when properly understood. "Cast them down to hell" represents a single word, *"tartarosas"*, which is, according to all the authorities, a verb indicating an action taking place at some specific point in time. The noun form of this word was used in pre-Christian mythology to describe the place where "rebellious gods" were incarcerated. It came to mean the deepest part of Hades. Since this is the only occasion where the word appears in the New Testament, it would be unwise to give it a meaning exclusively derived from a non-Biblical and superstitious origin. Peter's statement could be rendered, most awkwardly, "God spared not the angels that sinned but *'tartarosized'* them, delivering them into chains of darkness, to be reserved unto judgment". The words "delivering them into chains of darkness" would then explain Peter's use of the word *"tartaroo"*, which, if Jude had access to the epistle in question, he would recognize. Jude does appear to be in agreement with this view of Peter's teaching. The third part of both statements is also in complete accord. While Peter writes, "the angels that sinned are to be reserved unto judgment", Jude notes that God "hath reserved (them) until the judgment of the great day" (v.6).

## "Chains of Darkness"

The fact that "the chains of darkness" are taken to be metaphorical does not in any way lessen the dreadfulness of divine judgment imposed upon the angels that sinned. The "chains" speak of the awful condition into which Satan and his followers were cast as soon as they had committed the sin of rebellious apostasy and in which they remain under bondage to this present time. Such is the state of darkness in which they are held that not the slightest ray of light, nor of hope, can ever penetrate their gloom. Bound in this inescapable fashion they await the great day of judgment in the conscious and unalleviated knowledge that their eternal destiny is the lake of fire. Note the terror implied in the words of the demons to the Lord Jesus. "Art Thou come hither to torment us before the time?" (Matt 8.29). Few will see any reason to doubt that these words are connected to the demons' request in the parallel passage of Luke 8.31: "And they besought Him that He would not command them to go into the abyss".

Further, their darkness is so great that not even Satan himself can appreciate, to the slightest degree, the grace of salvation which enables a man to trust his God, no matter the consequences, in this present life. The book of Job fully illustrates this point. In gracious contrast to the judgment immediately overtaking the angels that sinned, the original sin of Adam and Eve drew forth a response from God which, though in outward form faint, was a lovely picture of God's purpose and plan for mankind. Sacrifice was made and nakedness was covered thus foretelling, in a typical manner, how the work of redemption was to be accomplished. The typical presentation thus begun in Eden has been called the 'proto-evangel', or 'first Gospel', and was continued throughout the whole of the OT finding its literal climax at Calvary, the Lord Jesus became "a little lower than the angels on account of the suffering of death". This He willingly undertook, not to lay hold of angels in redemption, but to take hold of Abraham's seed and fulfill in them the purposes of salvation (Gal 3.9,10). It is the redeemed out from among men He calls "My brethren" (Heb 2.9-16). From their own ranks, the holy angels witnessed countless numbers consigned to deep chains of gloom to await the dreadful day of judgment of being cast into the eternal lake of fire. They also see, in amazement, how the many-faceted grace of God lays hold of mortal man and raises him, in Christ, to a place of nearness no angel can ever enjoy. These majestic beings desire, with a holy curiosity, to fathom the depths of God's grace to men, but they never can experience, in themselves, what salvation's wonders are. The hymn writer has caught this note with exquisite sensitivity when he wrote:

'There is singing up in heaven such as we have never known,
As the angels chant their chorus to the Lamb upon the throne.
Their sweet harps are ever tuneful and their voices ever clear.
Oh, that we could be more like them as we serve the master here.
For, Holy, Holy, Holy, is what the angels sing,

*And I expect to help them make the courts of heaven ring.*
*But when I sing redemption's story, they must fold their*
  *wings,*
*For angels never knew the joy that my salvation brings.'*

CHAPTER 7

# The Demons

No study of angels, be it ever so short or selective, can be complete without some reference being made to "fallen angels". That such a term does not appear in Holy Scripture is evident enough, but other statements used by the Holy Spirit concerning the hosts of rebellious beings, amply warrants the use of the term to describe these creatures who are spoken of as "the devil's angels" (Matt 25.41; Rev 12.9).

While other divergent opinions do exist, it is generally accepted that the angels who originally joined with Satan in his defiance of God are the "demons" so often referred to in both Old and New Testaments. "The angels that sinned" (2 Pet 2.4) stand in dread contrast to the "angels of God" (Gen 28.12) in their character, activity and eventual destiny.

In previous chapters, it has been necessary to refer to these wicked creatures but, once again, we are facing a subject which occupying a very large place in Holy Writ is not as well understood as it should be. It warrants a closer look.

To be concise and, at the same time, orderly, the following four headings will help us understand this further important aspect of a complex subject.

The Identity of the Demons
The Activity of the Demons
The Purpose of the Demons
The Destiny of the Demons

**The Identity of the Demons**

The Word of God gives much more information about Satan and his character than it does about the angels who have offered him their allegiance. Satan is called by the Lord Jesus, "Beelzebub" (Matt 10.25) and as such, is designated "the prince of demons". The Lord also describes him as "the strong man" who must be bound before his house is entered and his goods spoiled (Matt 12.29). Attention has already been drawn to two titles given him; "the prince of this world" (John 12.31) and "the god of this world" (2 Cor 4.4). These scriptures combined show us the extent of Satan's authority and influence. He has at his command countless numbers of wicked angels of whom he is "the prince" and who form at least part of "his house". His influence for evil affects the whole of this world for "the whole world lies in wickedness", or, perhaps better, "lies in the lap of the Wicked One" (1 John 5.19, literal translation).

There are many in the world who deny the existence of both the devil and his angels. Generally speaking, such individuals do not acknowledge anything pertaining to the world of the spirit. In spite of this it cannot be denied that the belief in malicious and vicious beings, usually spoken of as "demons", is to be found in every land and in every age. Not only so, but man's experience teaches him that his world is not the happy and benign place he wishes it was. On every hand, there seem to be forces, most often beyond his ability to explain, that are destructive in nature. Such universal beliefs and experiences persist, the weight of so much religious philosophy denying the very existence of evil in men or in his society, notwithstanding. These beliefs and experiences cannot be dismissed as originating in mere ignorance and superstition. Too many people in too many lands and for too long a period of time have accepted the existence of the beings we speak of as demons for them to be merely the figment of unenlightened thought. Many are the theories as to their origin, but the Holy Scriptures give an unequivocal testimony as to their beginnings. Lucifer sought for himself the highest place in the universe (Isa 14.13). In his attempt to usurp that which was divine, he drew with him a numberless host of angelic beings, perhaps one-third of the unnumbered host created for the sole purpose of serving their Lord (Rev 12.4). These beings, turning from holy obedience to their Creator, gave to Satan their unrestrained co-operation for the fulfillment of his hellish ambition. That purpose was meant eventually to displace the Man of God's appointment on the Throne of the Most High. Neither Satan nor any of his minions are omniscient nor omnipresent, but the principle that "the gifts and calling of God are without repentance" (Rom 11.29) may surely be recognized, so that the angels, though fallen, remain far superior to men in their powers and intellect. Created in holiness to serve in perfection, by their inordinate pride and disobedience, the demons have become the angels of Satan and share with him an unmitigated hatred of everything that is holy.

## The Activity of the Demons

To the Western mind, idolatry, for the most part, appears to be something which flows from a different culture and is, at best, harmless and, at worst, simply superstition. However, the Scriptures of Truth give a more realistic view of such false worship. Idolatry, in its basic character, is a continuation of Satan's original desire to claim for himself what belongs to God alone. The apostle Paul goes to the heart of the matter in 1 Corinthians 10.20 when he writes, "the things which the Gentiles sacrifice, they sacrifice to demons and not to God". From ancient times, and universally, idol worship originated in demonic activity. The "doctrine of demons" consists of hypocritical lies, apostasy, the breaking down of the marriage bond, superficial religiosity and behaviour that results from a seared and scarred conscience. Another result is the supposed ability of certain men and women to delve into the world of the spirits (1 Tim 4.1-3). But this ability to reach into the spiritual realm has not been given to men, certainly not by God nor is it permitted by Him either. The witch of Endor, who was, ostensibly, a practitioner of such arts, was terrified when God actually allowed Samuel to return from the other world to make an appearance to Saul (1 Sam 28.7). It would appear that these last years of the twentieth century are heavily marked by such activity which, if genuine, the Scriptures ascribe to "Satan and his angels".

It has been noted that during the days of our Lord's sojourn among men, the activities of evil spirits were most marked. The Gospels abound with instances showing that various sicknesses were the work of these malicious beings. All illness may not be ascribed to their power, but one thing is sure, in their desire to disrupt and to destroy, they will use any means available to them. Their deep-seated desire to "possess" bodies of flesh and blood, even to the extent of requesting that they might be sent into the herd of swine (Luke 8.32), emphasizes the fact that they do not have the ability to change their own basic nature. Their desire to possess such bodies is not for sexual purposes, but to expedite and enlarge their work of destruction. Related to this subject is the question as to whether demon possession exists today. That it does, in different forms, very few intelligent readers of God's Word would doubt, but one thing is absolutely certain. No true believer can ever be possessed by demons. The Christian can be influenced and pressured by them from without, perhaps even to the extent of severe depression to an extremely unhealthy and self-destructive degree, but as a temple indwelt by the Holy Spirit of God, the believer is far beyond the reach of these beings who wish to possess a body for their own devious purposes. Destructive powers are at their disposal, but ultimate success is not.

**The Purpose of the Demons**
Their object is only too clear. It is two-fold. Firstly they would thwart the divine purpose in every way possible and

also they would extend the authority of their prince with all the powers of their beings. God's eternal design is that a Man might reign eternally and universally; that Man, "Lord Sabaoth is His Name", to quote Luther's magnificent hymn. The heavenly decree has gone forth with regards to that Man, "Sit Thou at My right hand until I make Thine enemies Thy footstool" (Ps 110.1). Regardless of all their devilish activity the Lord Jesus shall reign until all His enemies are under His feet, and a trumpet will send forth the universal declaration "the kingdoms of this world are become the Kingdom of our Lord, and His Christ" (Rev 11.15). In that day the strains of Handel's "Hallelujah Chorus", which may thrill the believer to the depth of his being today, will sound, to some degree, like an amateurish attempt to express the inexpressible.

## The Final Doom of the Demons

For beings of such great potential, their ultimate destination is a source of fathomless sorrow. Remember how, with deep sadness, the Lord Jesus said, "I beheld Satan as lightning fall from heaven" (Luke 10.18). Whether these words can be interpreted as to Satan's past history or to that time in the future when he will be cast out of heaven, is not at all clear. It may be that they apply even to the time then present when the demons had become subject to mere mortals in the ministry of the apostles. In what ever way they are interpreted the profound pathos that the Lord's words evoke serves to emphasize the awfulness of what awaits Satan and his followers: "Everlasting fire, prepared for the devil and his angels" (Matt 25.41). From the loftiest heights of created grandeur, to the fathomless depths of eternal doom; no rest, no peace, no light, no joy and, worst of all, no hope for evermore. But for the matchless, limitless grace of our God, we, too, would have shared their awful doom in hell and the eternal lake of fire. Instead, we raise our voices with Murray McCheyne and sing:

'When the praise of heaven I hear, loud as thunders to the
   ear,
Loud as many waters' noise; sweet as harp's melodious
   voice:
Then, Lord, shall I fully know, not till then how much I
   owe.
Chosen not for good in me; wakened up from wrath to
   flee;
Hidden in the Saviour's side; by the Spirit sanctified.
Teach me, Lord, on earth to show by my love, how much
   I owe.'

CHAPTER 8

# "The Sons of God" (Genesis 6)

Few passages of Scripture lend themselves to controversy as much as the early verses of Genesis 6. Spiritual and capable men have ranged themselves on both sides of the argument that is not by any means of recent origin. When learned men of good intention differ, rude dogmatism is very unbecoming. Nevertheless, a positive statement as to the meaning of such a passage of God's Word is not out of place in this short study, but a fair and, if possible, an unprejudiced approach to the problem is necessary.

## Two Explanations
One of the two widely accepted explanations of these well known verses is that "the sons of God" (Gen 6.2) were angels who, being attracted by the beauty of "the daughters of men", that is, women in the ordinary sense of the word, contracted a sensual and unnatural relationship with them. The result of these unlawful liaisons was that "there were giants in the earth in those days", these being the progeny of the angels and their consorts. The issue of such co-habitation was then spoken of as "mighty men which were of old, men of renown" (Gen 6.4).

In support of this view, which has had many scholarly advocates, three New Testament references are brought forth. Two of these Scriptures have already been touched upon and an attempt made to explain them.

They now must be considered in the light of the preceding paragraph. The first of these references is found in 2 Peter 2.4 where Peter speaks of the angels that sinned: whom God did not spare but "cast them down to hell and delivered them into chains of darkness to be reserved unto judgment". Secondly, in Jude's epistle, these same angels are designated as those "which kept not their first estate but left their own habitation, He (the Lord) hath reserved in everlasting chains under darkness unto the judgment of the great day" (v.6). Finally, Peter's words once again are referred to in support of this view. "Christ ... being put to death in the flesh but quickened by the Spirit; by which also He went and preached unto the spirits in prison; which sometimes were disobedient in the days of Noah" (1 Peter 3.19, 20).

Taken together, these three portions of God's Word are explained as follows. In the period prior to the flood of Noah's day, certain angels, aggravating the original sin of Satan and his followers in rebellion, committed further and, probably in a personal way, a more devastating evil which is described as "leaving their own habitation (principality)". This they did by co-habiting with women of their choice. The fearful result, given as an awe inspiring example in the writings of Peter and Jude, is that they have been consigned to a special incarceration spoken of as being "cast-down- to-hell (tartaroas)" (2 Pet 2.4) where they have been "delivered to chains (or pits) of darkness and reserved unto the judgment of the great day". Whatever their being "cast-down-to-hell" may be taken to mean, their deliverance to these "chains of darkness" is indeed a fearful example of the judgment of a holy God against sin. To these beings, thus incarcerated, the Lord Jesus is said to have gone, during the three days in which His body lay in the grave and, in spirit, He proclaimed His mighty victory over sin and Satan at the cross. This is believed to be a fair, though brief, statement of what many teach with regard to these verses of Genesis 6 now under consideration. Not all who subscribe to the view thus expressed will be happy with every thing as here stated. That will be understood, of course.

Opposing this idea is the view that "the sons of God" were the descendants of Seth who, being physically attracted to "the daughters of men", that is women from the families of Cain's descendants, "took them wives of all which they choose" (Gen 6.2). In general, a clearly marked line of demarcation had been drawn by the two groups of Adam's offspring, one by following in the wicked footsteps of Cain (N.B. Gen 4.17-24), and the other by following the steps of Abel and Enoch "calling upon the name of the Lord" (4.26). But the boundary line of separation was erased by the mingling of these two family groups. This was particularly so because the "men" of the generally "godly line" became completely infatuated with the daughters of the ungodly to the extent of marrying all they set their minds upon. They were thus imitating Lamech who began the practice of polygamy (4.19) contrary to the revealed will of God (Gen 2.24). This resulted in an even greater and wholesale departure from God and His ways. Man corrupted the earth with his wickedness and was consequently destroyed by the flood. This explanation appears to be more in keeping with the context as found in Genesis 6, especially if for the sake of the context the beginning of ch.6 is directly linked with the last words of ch.4. For that reason, this second explanation is the one supported in handling the subject here. Further consideration is called for.

## Were the "Sons of God" angels?

It cannot be denied that this view has many ancient

proponents, including the translators of the Septuagint (Greek) version of the Old Testament. Those responsible (72 Jewish scholars) actually saw fit to use the interpretation "angels of God" to express the original words *bene elohim*. That the writer of the apocryphal book of Enoch together with Josephus, the historian, also held this view, further shows its antiquity. Since the Septuagint was the version in use in the days of the Lord Jesus, it has been suggested that it was likely the view held by both Jewish commentators and the very earliest Christian writers. Lessening the force of this apparently strong argument is the fact that from much more ancient times, myths and legends existed which suggested a union between "demigods" (angels or other spirit beings) and human women. It is very possible that a whole generation of otherwise godly men could be influenced in their thinking by ideas which had received almost universal acceptance in the society of their day. (Note by way of illustration how, from the introduction of Darwinistic evolutionary thinking in the nineteenth century until relatively recent times, a vast number of Christian writers in western lands supported what they believed to be a scriptural accommodation to this God-defaming philosophy). Further, a correct interpretation of this or any other passage of God's Word must have recourse to the original Scriptures and not merely to a translation, especially one such as the Septuagint marked as it is by many indifferent interpretations.

The exact phrase *bene elohim* is found three times in Job (1.6; 2.1; 38.7) where, clearly, the angels of God are meant. This fact does indeed give strength to the belief that in Genesis 6, the words also indicate supernatural beings. To surmount this difficulty, some writers have attempted, without much success, to explain these 'sons of God' in Job 2 as being godly men coming before the Lord in worship. No less an exegete of Scripture than Sidlow Baxter sets forth this explanation in detail, but the reference in Job 38 does not appear to allow such an interpretation. However, similar phrases indicating believing mankind are found throughout the Old Testament with the exact equivalent in the language of the Greek New Testament. That the same phrase is used to describe angels in their relationship to their Creator and, at the same time, to set forth the intimate and privileged one the believer enjoys with his God by virtue of the redemptive process, is not, by any means, a thing to be thought strange. Perhaps the reason why OT saints were not given the uncluttered title of *bene elohim* was that their full standing of liberty and grace awaited the fuller revelation of the NT while the angels already enjoyed that standing by virtue of creation. The use of the term in Genesis 6 would then be explained by the fact that, for the first time, men, and godly men at that, openly called upon God in collective public worship.

That the interpretation of these verses in Genesis 6 depends on the meaning of the phrase "sons of God" is quite clear. But to arrive at the true meaning, other Scriptures also need to be considered. Later reference will be made to some of these so that a clearer understanding may be reached.

A tolerant approach must be taken by all who would write about, or in any other way, seek to expound this subject. But one note of caution must be offered to any who see in the "sons of God" of Genesis 6 a miraculous acquiring by angels of some form of humanity to enable them to co-habit with woman kind. Does this explanation not encroach upon the absolute uniqueness of the Lord's incarnation? If, after all, mere created beings, such as are the angels, are able to assume at will virtual humanity for their nefarious purpose, then the taking of humanity into Deity by the Lord Jesus is not to be marveled at in the least - since scores of angels have, by their own volition, procured for themselves bodies of flesh and blood. Apart from the birth process which was the Lord's special experience, the Incarnation can then no longer be termed unique. In spite of what Paul wrote, "inexplicably great is the mystery of godliness, God was manifest in flesh" (1 Tim 3.16) there is now nothing outstandingly remarkable about the Diety becoming man since angels already had, apparently, been capable of doing something very similar. But this anticipates what is to follow.

**Further Objections to the "Angels" Explanation**

   To teach that, at one stage in the history of the world, angels co-habited with women, is to claim for them an ability which is not given to creatures, no matter how exalted, but is reserved for the Creator alone, that is, the ability to change their own essential nature or to create a new one for themselves. Speaking of the resurrection state, the Lord Jesus made a definitive comment: "They neither marry nor are given in marriage but are as the angels of God in heaven" (Matt 22.30). These words describing, negatively, the resurrection state and, equally, that of the "angels of God in heaven", are exactly the same as used by the Lord of the people of Noah's day, "marrying and giving in marriage" (Matt 24. 38). In referring to that generation and its characteristic godless existence, the Lord gave not the slightest intimation of an incursion of other worldly beings into man's society. Nor can the words "the angels of God *in heaven*" be used to weaken the objection proposed. Were the "angels who sinned" not "in heaven" (or being of a heavenly abode) prior to their taking some manner of human form, if such is the case? Were they not at that time "angels of God"? If they were, then it can be said of them, and of all their fellows, "they neither marry nor are given in marriage".

Angels have appeared in human form on various occasions. This is evident to all readers of the Scriptures, but these appearances were that, appearances only. The angels on their divinely appointed commissions did not become men, but for a time, assumed the appearance of men. This is vastly different to what is taught with regards to "the sons of God" in the passage under discussion. There is a parallel which further mitigates against this teaching. If we allow that "the Angel of the Lord", who appeared numerous times in human form was the pre-incarnate Christ, does that mean that the body or bodily form He assumed at the time would have been capable of experiencing death? Surely not. If this were so then in these pre-incarnate appearances the Lord Jesus would have taken to Himself virtual humanity. This is manifestly not the case. Angels, then, commissioned to wait upon men in their service for God, in the same fashion, only assumed, as divinely commissioned, a temporary human appearance for the purpose of revelation.

It is readily admitted, even by many who accept the view that these "sons of God" were angels, that the idea of them changing their basic nature into something their Creator never intended, is not easily understood. If they did what they are said to have done, then they, in actual fact, created for themselves an entirely new mode of existence. To support such a breathtaking event on tenuous arguments, appears to go beyond the bounds of sound interpretation. Recognizing this in-surmountable difficulty some writers have recourse to the "demon possession" theory. This means that the "sons of God" were actual men but possessed by demons for the purpose of wiping out the godly seed. Again, this hellish purpose is not to be denied as the satanic object in any age is to do just that, but to appeal to such an idea does not do justice to the relevant Scriptures.

The words of the Lord Jesus already referred to above, imply that what happened in Noah's day will be repeated in the days immediately prior to the coming of the Son of Man. If we take the words literally, (and is there any reason why we should not?), then surely the conditions to be duplicated at the end times demand a further incursion of angelic beings to "take them wives of all which they choose" - that is, if angels were indeed involved in the original "marrying and giving in marriage". Not only so, but if, as is taught, "giants" were the result of these unholy liaisons, were there other occasions when such ungodly "marriages" took place? If not, from whence do the "giants" of later periods spring? Note, for example, Numbers 13.33 and Deuteronomy 2.10,20,21. "Giants" appear at different times in both Biblical and secular history. Note, however, that the wording of Genesis 6.4 does not, in any way, demand that their existence be explained by an unnatural alliance between angels and the "daughters of men".

## A Contextual Explanation

Genesis 4 contains the record of Abel's murder by his brother Cain. Then is given Cain's genealogy, which encompasses a mere seven generations from Cain to Tubal-cain. Finally, the birth of Seth, to take Abel's place, is noted with the interesting comment "then men began to call upon the name of the Lord" (Gen 4.26). The murder of Abel is calculated to show Cain for what he was, a man of violence. The genealogy, in seven generations from Cain to Tubal-cain, underscores the fact that "that which is born of the flesh is flesh", while the words of Lamech (vv.23-24) prove that Cain's descendants also are marked by ruthlessness and violence. These are the very things characterizing the days prior to the Flood and because of which the judgment of God engulfed the earth. But, separated from the godless line, there were men who "called upon the name of the Lord" in the beginnings of their approach to God in a more ritualistic form of worship. Chapter 5 traces this line in the children of Seth. To say that every one of these descendants was godly would be going beyond what the Scripture has shown, but in contrast to the violence which marked Cain's progeny and became characteristic of the world at that time this other line of descendants, as noted in ch.5, was marked by a "calling upon the name of the Lord". This is seen in the meaning of the names from Adam to Noah as recorded there. A tracing of the God of Glory in His dealings with frail, mortal man for his salvation and comfort appears to be encoded. Thus, the two families are clearly distinguished, one infamous in its lawlessness, and the other evidencing a reverence for God.

Such distinctions are immediately done away with at the beginning of ch.6 as "the sons of God saw the daughters of men that they were fair; and they took them wives of all that they choose". The children of such unions were spoken of as "mighty men which were of old, men of renown". Men marked by wickedness who, apparently, filled the earth with violence in keeping with the character of some of their forefathers. Genesis 6.4 does not state these children were the giants, but that "there were giants in the land" at the time these events took place, and "also after that". That is to say, after the co-habitating of the two families took place, among the resulting children, there were mighty men, wicked men of renown. Then the author of Genesis gives us an added feature characterizing those days preceding the flood. There were giants in the land at that time. When, in later ages, giants appear from time to time, this would be the result of the natural gene pool found in mankind which, on occasions, produces such men even to this day. Genesis 6 merely states that they were more in evidence in the days immediately prior to the flood. This, by the way, is completely in keeping with what is now known about the pre-Noahican world. The fossil record shows that "giantism" was prevalent in both the animal and vegetable spheres. There is no need to propose a co-habiting of angels and women to explain the fact there were "giants in the earth in those days".

**Other Relevant Scriptures**

The words of Jude, "the angels which kept not their first estate (or principality), but left their own habitation" may be applied equally well to either of the views considered here. If "the sons of God" in Genesis 6 are interpreted as being angels, then these words may easily be linked to them. But they can also, with equal force, be used with regards to the angels who joined Satan in his original rebellion. It is said of Satan in Ezekiel 28.18, "thou hast defiled thy sanctuaries", a statement just as easily connected with the words "kept not their first estate but left their habitation". Peter calls this group of beings "the angels that sinned" (2 Pet 2.4). It is hardly likely that he would refer in this unadorned description to those creatures who, in a sense, committed the lesser transgression, when the "angels that sinned" together with Satan, in their original rebellion actually opened the floodgates for all manner of wickedness, including that of gross immorality, in God's creation. It has, of course, been suggested that "in going after strange flesh" in the same manner as Sodom and Gomorrah, the angels actually did leave their "first estate". Note, it is the citizens of these cities, we are told, who went after "strange flesh", not the angels. These words are in keeping with the type of wickedness marking their communities but out of place in the realm of spirits "which do not have a body of flesh and bones" (Luke 24.39), unless they were capable of creating physical bodies in order to fulfill their lusts. By way of contrast, it may be stated that Satan's lusts had an upward thrust. He left his own principality by aiming at one much higher and one beyond his reach in the throne of the Most High. Scripture records many instances of demon (fallen angel) possession but never one for the sole purpose of sexual gratification. Even in their fallen state, "angels" appear to have no tendencies to this evil, but may encourage men to gratify their fleshly desires unlawfully, simply because such deeds, along with all such wickedness, constitute disobedience to and rebellion against God.

The sentence in Jude, "Even as Sodom and Gomorrah ... in like manner" does not refer to the sin of these cities, but to the fact that they, along with the angels who sinned, are set forth as fearful examples of the inescapable judgment of God against all manner of iniquity. A corrected reading making this point very clear would be, "Even as Sodom and Gomorrah and the cities about them, giving themselves to fornication and going after strange flesh, are in like manner as these angels, set forth as an example, suffering the vengeance of eternal fire". In 2 Peter, the same purpose may be seen; that of the example of the people of Noah's day, the cities of the plain, and the sinning angels in the judgments they received.

Repeatedly in Genesis 6, men are looked upon as the cause of the earth being filled with violence and they alone are held responsible for the resulting catastrophe. Thus, it would be strange if, in fact, angelic beings were the instigators of such wickedness and that in the face of greater standing and privilege. It would seem best to accept the interpretation, held by many conservative students of the Word in different ages and cultures, that these "sons of God" were the progeny of the Seth family who, leaving a path marked by a large measure of God fearingness, by their resulting lustful actions, broke down the divine line of demarcation and thus incurred the outpouring of God's wrath against sin. Man's history, as we all know, has ever been marked by just such departure and sin.

**Conclusion**

In following, even in a superficial way, what the Word of God has to say about "angels" we are brought face to face with two fundamentally important facts.

(1) The unbending holiness and righteousness of God demand that evil be put away, either by sacrifice or by judgment.

(2) God has, on the grounds of immeasurable righteousness, procured a means of redemption "whereby His banished be not expelled from Him" (2 Sam 14.14).

The song of praise has already begun on earth; not the song of angels but that of redeemed men. It will echo through the unending ages of eternity and it is:

*"Unto Him that loved us, and washed us from our sins in His own blood, and hath made us kings and priests unto God and His Father; to Him be glory and dominion for ever and ever, Amen"* (Rev 1.5-6).

# Bibliography

Alders, G.H.; *Bible Student's Commentary, Vol.1, 'Genesis'* (Zondervan)

Allen, J.; *What the Bible Teaches, Vol. 9 Revelation* (J. Ritchie Ltd.)

Chafer, Lewis Sperry; *Systematic Theology, Vol. 2* (Dunham Pub. Co.)

Gabelein, A.C.; *What the Bible Says About Angels* (Baker)

Green, Michael; Tyndale Commentaries, *2nd Peter & Jude* (Tyndale Press)

Harrison, Roland K.; *Introduction to the OT* (Erdman's Pub.Co.)

Jennings, F.C.; *Satan, His Person & Work, Place & Destiny* (Loizeaux Bros)

Jeremiah, David; *What the Bible Says About Angels* (Multinomah Press)

Kelly, Wm.; *The Serious Christian, Vol.1 Jude*

Manton, Thos.; *The Epistle of Jude* (Banner of Truth Trust)

McDonald, Wm.; *Believer's Bible Commentary, OT & NT* (Nelson)

McShane, A.; *What the Bible Teaches, Vol.5 Jude* (J. Ritchie Ltd.)

Needham, Mrs. Geo. C.; *Angels & Demons* (Moody Press)

Stier, Rudolf; *The Words of Angels* (1886 Publication)

Strauss, Lehman; *Demons, Yes but Thank God for Good Angels* (Loizeaux Bros.)

Unger, Merril F.; *Biblical Demonology* (Scripture Press)

Vine, W.E.; *Expository Dictionary of OT & NT Words* (Revell)

Various Authors *The Biblical Expositor, Vol. 1* (Baker Book House)

Waugh, G.P.; *What the Bible Teaches Vol. 5, 2nd Peter* (J. Ritchie Ltd.)

# Scripture Index

HOSEA
1.10    14

MALACHI
3.1    30

NEW TESTAMENT

MATTHEW
1.20    42
4.11    42
8.29    52
9.34    26
10.25   56
12.29   56
13.11   10
20.28   30
22.30   14,66
24.38   66
25.31   17
25.41   55,59
26.53   15

LUKE
1.9     30
1.11    19
1.41    11
2.13    14
8.31    52
8.32    58
10.18   59
12.8    37
15.10   41,47
22.43   42
24.39   15,71

JOHN
1.14    30
1.18    22
1.51    33

3.16    18
12.31   56
14.30   26
17.1    18

ACTS
3.15    26
7.53    32

ROMANS
1.20    7
11.29   57
11.33   47

1 CORINTHIANS
3.8     38
4.9-13  47
10.20   57
11.3    44
11.5    36
11.5-16 36
11.10   34,41,46
14.37   37

2 CORINTHIANS
4.4     56
12.14   22

GALATIANS
3.9,10  53
3.19    32
3.28    35
4.6     14

EPHESIANS
1.5-9   43
2.1-3   43
2.2     26
2.7     43
2.10    43

2.20,21  43
2.23     43
3.8      44
3.10     34,41,43

PHILIPPIANS
1.7      51
2.5-11   17,42
2.7,8    17
3.21     15

COLOSSIANS
1.13-17  16
1.16     26,44
1.25     43
2.9      23

1 THESSALONIANS
4.16     37
5.23     14

2 THESSALONIANS
1.7      31

1 TIMOTHY
2.11-12  35
2.14     35
3.6      17
3.16     17,33,34,41,42,66
4.1-3    57
5.21     17,37,39,46

2 TIMOTHY
3.16,17  9

HEBREWS
1.4,5    18
1.6      16,37
1.8      19